THE SIMPLE WISDOM OF
POPE FRANCIS

OUR HEART'S
DESIRE

Libreria Editrice Vaticana

United States Conference of Catholic Bishops
Washington, DC

First printing, July 2014

ISBN 978-1-60137-472-1

CONTENTS

INTRODUCTION

You have in your possession one of the volumes of *The Simple Wisdom of Pope Francis* series, the first compilation of Pope Francis's teachings.

Immediately after his election on March 13th 2013, the world turned their eyes to the new Successor of Peter to notice Pope Francis's simple ways, humbleness, and his love for the poor and the sick.

This collection captures the wisdom of Pope Francis during his general audiences, which are regularly held on Wednesdays when the pope is in Rome. The general audiences give pilgrims and visitors a chance to "see the pope" and receive the Papal Blessing, or Apostolic Blessing, from the successor of the Apostle Peter. General audiences with the pope are spoken mainly in Italian, but also in English, French, Spanish, or other languages depending on the groups visiting. They consist of short, scripturally-based teachings in which the pope instructs the faithful across the world.

It is our prayer that the teachings of the Holy Father within this series will be a source of hope and help in embracing the grace of faith a little more each day.

GOD'S LOVE IS TRUE WEALTH

AUGUST 4, 2013

ST. PETER'S SQUARE

Dear Brothers and Sisters,

Last Sunday I was in Rio de Janeiro. Holy Mass and the World Youth Day were drawing to a close. I think we must all thank the Lord together for the great gift which this event was, for Brazil, for Latin America and for the entire world. It was a new stage on the pilgrimage of youth crossing the continents bearing the Cross of Christ. We must never forget that World Youth Days are not "firework displays," flashes of enthusiasm that are an end in themselves; they are the stages of a long journey, begun in 1985, at the initiative of Pope John Paul II. He entrusted the cross to the young people and said: go out and I will come with you! And so

1

it was; and this youth pilgrimage continued with Pope Benedict and, thanks be to God, I too have been able to experience this marvellous milestone in Brazil. Let us always remember: young people do not follow the Pope, they follow Jesus Christ, bearing his Cross. And the Pope guides them and accompanies them on this journey of faith and hope. I therefore thank all the young people who have taken part, even at the cost of sacrifices. I also thank the Lord for the other encounters I had with the Pastors and people of that vast country which Brazil is, and likewise the authorities and the volunteers. May the Lord reward all those who worked hard for the success of this great feast of faith. I also want to emphasize my gratitude; many thanks to the Brazilians. The people of Brazil are an excellent people, a people with a great heart! I shall not forget the warm welcome, the greetings, their gaze, all the joy. A generous people; I ask the Lord to shower his blessings upon them!

....

Let us always remember: young people do not follow the Pope, they follow Jesus Christ, bearing his Cross.

I would like to ask you to pray with me that the young people who took part in World Youth Day will be able to express this experience in their journey through daily life, in their everyday conduct; and that they can also express it in the important decisions of life, in response to the personal call of the Lord. Today in the liturgy, the provocative words of Ecclesiastes ring out: "Vanity of vanities! All is vanity!" (1:2). Young people are particularly sensitive to the empty, meaningless values that often surround them. Unfortunately, moreover, it is they who pay the consequences. Instead the encounter with the living Christ in his great family which is the Church fills hearts with joy, for it fills them with true life, with a profound goodness that endures, that does not tarnish. We saw it on the faces of the youth in Rio. But this experience must confront the daily vanity, that poison of emptiness which creeps into our society based on profit and possession and on consumerism which deceives young people. This Sunday's Gospel reminds us, precisely, of the absurdity of basing our own happiness on having. The rich say to themselves: my soul, you have many possessions at your disposal . . . rest, eat, drink and be merry! But God says to them: Fools! This very night your life will be required of you. And all the things you have accumulated, whose will they be? (cf. Lk 12:19-20).

Dear brothers and sisters, the true treasure is the love of God shared with our brethren. That love which comes from God and enables us to share it with one another and to help each other. Those who experience it do not fear death and their hearts are at peace. Let us entrust this intention, the intention of receiving God's love and sharing it with our brothers and sisters, to the intercession of the Blessed Virgin Mary.

❧

Dear Brothers and Sisters,

I greet you all and I thank you for your presence despite the heat. . . .

My thanks to you all! There are lots of young people in the Square today! It's like Rio de Janeiro!

I would like to assure you of my special remembrance for parish priests and for all the priests in the world because today we are commemorating their Patron, St. John Mary Vianney. Dear confreres, let us be united in prayer and in pastoral charity.

Tomorrow as Romans we commemorate our Mother, the *Salus Populi Romani*: let us ask her to protect us; and now, all together, let us greet her with a *Hail Mary*. All together, "Hail Mary. . . ." A greeting to our Mother, all together, a greeting to the Mother! (*He applauds with the people*).

I am also pleased to remember the liturgical Feast of the Transfiguration which will be the day after tomorrow, with a thought of deep gratitude for Venerable Pope Paul VI, who departed this life on the evening of August 6, thirty-five years ago.

Dear friends, I wish you a good Sunday and a good month of August. And a good lunch! Goodbye!

A YEARNING HEART

AUGUST 11, 2013

ST. PETER'S SQUARE

Dear Brothers and Sisters, good morning!

This Sunday's Gospel (Lk 12:32-48) speaks to us about the desire for the definitive encounter with Christ, a desire that keeps us ever ready, alert in spirit, for we anticipate this encounter with all our heart, with all our being. This is a fundamental aspect of life. It is a desire that we all share, whether explicit or secret, we have hidden in our heart; we all harbor this desire in our heart.

It is also important to see Jesus' teaching in the actual context in which he transmitted it. In this case, Luke the Evangelist shows us Jesus walking with his disciples to Jerusalem, walking to his death and resurrection at Easter, and on this journey he teaches them, confiding to them what he himself carries in his heart, the deep attitude of his heart: detachment from earthly possessions,

5

his trust in the Father's Providence and, indeed, his innermost watchfulness, all the while working for the Kingdom of God. For Jesus it is waiting for his return to the Father's house. For us it is waiting for Christ himself who will come to take us to the everlasting celebration, as he did for his Mother, Mary Most Holy; he took her up to Heaven with him.

The Gospel intends to tell us that the Christian is someone who has a great desire, a deep desire within him: to meet his Lord with his brothers and sisters, his travelling companions. And what Jesus tells us is summed up in his famous phrase: "For where your treasure is, there will your heart be also" (Lk 12:34). A heart full of desire.

> **Do you all have a desiring heart? A heart that desires?**

We all have desires. The poor ones are those who have no desire, no desire to go forward, toward the horizon; and for us Christians this horizon is the encounter with Jesus, the very encounter with him, who is our life, our joy, our happiness. I would like to ask you two questions. First: do you all have a desiring heart? A heart that desires? Think about it and respond silently in your hearts. I ask you is your heart filled with desire, or is it a closed heart, a sleeping heart, a heart numb to the things of life? The desire to go forward to encounter Jesus. The second question: where is your treasure, what are you longing for? Jesus told us: where your treasure is, there will be your heart—and I ask you: where is your treasure? What is the most important reality for you, the most precious reality, the one that attracts your heart like a magnet? What attracts your heart? May I say that it is God's love? Do you wish to do good to others, to live for the Lord and for your brothers and sisters? May I say this? Each one answer in his own heart. But someone could tell me: Father, I am someone who works, who has a family, for me the most important reality is to keep my family and work going. . . . Certainly, this is true, it is important. But what is the power that unites the family? It is indeed love, and the One who sows love in our hearts is God, God's love, it is precisely God's love that gives meaning to our small daily tasks and helps us face the great trials. This is the true treasure of humankind: going forward in life with love, with that love which the Lord has sown in our hearts, with God's love. This is the true treasure. But what is God's love? It is not something vague, some generic feeling. God's love has a name and a face: Jesus Christ, Jesus. Love for God is made manifest in Jesus. For we cannot love air. . . . Do we love air? Do

> **It is God's love that gives meaning to our small daily tasks and helps us face the great trials.**

we love all things? No, no we cannot, we love people and the person we love is Jesus, the gift of the Father among us. It is a love that gives value and beauty to everything else; a love that gives strength to the family, to work, to study, to friendship, to art, to all human activity. It even gives meaning to negative experiences, because this love allows us to move beyond these experiences, to go beyond them, not to remain prisoners of evil, it moves us beyond, always opening us to hope, that's it! Love of God in Jesus always opens us to hope, to that horizon of hope, to the final horizon of our pilgrimage. In this way our labors and failures find meaning. Even our sin finds meaning in the love of God because this love of God in Jesus Christ always forgives us. He loves us so much that he always forgives us.

Dear brothers and sisters, in the Church today we are commemorating St. Clare of Assisi who, in the footsteps of Francis, left everything to consecrate herself to Christ in poverty. St. Clare gives us a very beautiful testimony of today's Gospel reading: may she, together with the Virgin Mary, help us to live the Gospel, each one of us according to one's own vocation.

Dear brothers and sisters, we remember that this Thursday is the Solemnity of the Assumption of Mary. Let us think about Our Mother who arrived in Heaven with Jesus and on that day we celebrate her.

I would like to greet the Muslims of the whole world, our brothers and sisters, who recently celebrated the end of the month of Ramadan, dedicated in a special way to fasting, prayer and almsgiving. As I wrote in my message for this occasion, I hope that all Christians and Muslims will work to promote mutual respect especially through the education of the new generations.

I greet with affection all the Romans and pilgrims present. Today I also have the joy of greeting various youth groups . . . I also repeat to you the words which were the theme of the great meeting in Rio: "Go and make disciples of all nations."

To you all and to everyone, I wish a happy Sunday and a good lunch! Goodbye!

EVERY "YES" TO GOD IS A STEP TOWARD HEAVEN

Solemnity of the Assumption of the

Blessed Virgin Mary

August 15, 2013

Castel Gandolfo

Dear Brothers and Sisters,

At the end of this Celebration let us turn to the Virgin Mary in the prayer of the Angelus. Mary's journey to heaven began with the "yes" spoken in Nazareth in response to the Heavenly Messenger's announcement of God's will to her. And in reality it is just like this: every "yes" to God is a step toward Heaven, toward eternal life.

Because this is what the Lord wants: that all his children may have life in abundance! God wants us all with him, in his house!

Sadly, distressing news is coming from Egypt. I want to assure all the victims and their families, the wounded and all those suffering, of my prayers. Let us pray together for peace, for dialogue, for reconciliation in that beloved land and throughout the world. Mary, Queen of Peace, pray for us! Let us all say: Mary, Queen of Peace, pray for us!

I wish to remember the twenty-fifth anniversary of the Apostolic Letter *Mulieris Dignitatem*, of Blessed Pope John Paul II, on the dignity and vocation of women. This document is rich in ideas that deserve to be taken up again and developed; and at the base of it all is the figure of Mary. In fact, it came out during the Marian Year. Let us make our own the prayer at the end of this Apostolic Letter (cf. no. 31): so that, by meditat-

Every "yes" to God is a step toward Heaven, toward eternal life.

ing on the biblical mystery of womanhood, concentrated in Mary, all women may find their dignity and the fullness of their vocation, and that the Church as a whole may deepen and better understand the very great and important role of women.

I thank everyone present, the inhabitants of Castel Gandolfo and the pilgrims! I thank you and the inhabitants of Castel Gandolfo, thank you very much! . . . And all the pilgrims, especially those from Guinea with their Bishop. I greet with affection the alumni of the Passionist College "Michael Ham" from Vicente López, Argentina; as well as the young people from the Musical Band of the *Colegio José de Jesús Rebolledo* from Coatepec, Mexico.

And now, let us pray together to Our Lady . . .

I wish you a happy feast today, the Day of Our Lady: have a happy feast day and a good lunch!

OUR GAZE FIXED ON JESUS

AUGUST 18, 2013

ST. PETER'S SQUARE

Dear Brothers and Sisters, good morning!

In today's liturgy we listen to these words from the Letter to the Hebrews: "Let us run with perseverance the race that is set before us, looking to Jesus the pioneer and perfecter of our faith" (Heb 12:1-2). We must give special emphasis to this affirmation in this *Year of Faith*. Let us too, throughout this Year, keep our gaze fixed on Jesus because faith, which is our "yes" to the filial relationship with God, comes from him, comes from Jesus. He is the only mediator of this relationship between us and our Father who is in heaven. Jesus is the Son and we are sons in him.

This Sunday, however, the word of God also contains a word of Jesus which alarms us and must be explained, for otherwise it could give rise to misunderstanding. Jesus says to his disciples: "Do you think that I have come to give peace on earth? No, I tell you, but rather division" (Lk 12:51). What does this mean? It means that faith is not a decorative or ornamental element; living faith does not mean decorating life with a little religion, as if it were a cake and we were decorating it with cream. No, this is not faith. Faith means choosing God as the criterion and basis of life, and God is not empty, God is not neutral, God is always positive, God is love, and

> God is not empty, God is not neutral, God is always positive, God is love, and love is positive!

love is positive! After Jesus has come into the world it is impossible to act as if we do not know God, or as if he were something that is abstract, empty, a purely nominal reference. No, God has a real face, he has a name: God is mercy, God is faithfulness, he is life which is given to us all. For this reason Jesus says "I came to bring division." It is not that Jesus wishes to split people up. On the contrary Jesus is our peace, he is our reconciliation! But this peace is not the peace of the tomb, it is not neutrality, Jesus does not bring neutrality, this peace is not a compromise at all costs. Following Jesus entails giving up evil and selfishness and choosing good, truth and justice, even when this demands sacrifice and the renunciation of our own interests. And this indeed divides; as we know, it even cuts the closest ties. However, be careful: it is not Jesus who creates division! He establishes the criterion: whether to live for ourselves or to live for God and for others; to be served or to serve; to obey one's own ego or to obey God. It is in this sense that Jesus is a "sign that is spoken against" (Lk 2:34).

This word of the Gospel does not therefore authorize the use of force to spread the faith. It is exactly the opposite: the Christian's real force is the force of truth and of love, which involves renouncing all forms of violence. Faith and violence are incompatible! Instead, faith and strength go together. Christians are not violent; they are strong. And with what kind of strength? That of meekness, the strength of meekness, the strength of love.

Dear friends, even among Jesus' relatives there were some who at a certain point did not share his way of life and preaching, as the Gospel tells us (cf. Mk 3:20-21). His Mother, however, always followed him faithfully, keeping the eyes of her heart fixed on Jesus, the Son of the Most High, and on his mystery. And in the end, thanks to Mary's faith, Jesus' relatives became part of the first Christian community (cf. Acts 1:14). Let us ask Mary to help us too to keep our gaze firmly fixed on Jesus and to follow him always, even when it costs what it may.

Remember this: following Jesus is not neutral, following Jesus means being involved, because faith is not a superficial decoration, it is a strength of the soul!

Dear brothers and sisters, I greet you all with affection, Romans and pilgrims: families, parish groups, young people. . . .

I would like to ask you for a prayer for the victims of the ferry that sank in the Philippines, and also for the families . . . what great suffering!

Let us also continue to pray for peace in Egypt. All together: Mary, Queen of Peace, pray for us! Everyone (*he repeats with the people*): Mary, Queen of Peace, pray for us! . . .

I wish you all a good Sunday and a good lunch! Goodbye!

JESUS IS THE DOOR TO SALVATION

AUGUST 25, 2013

ST. PETER'S SQUARE

Dear Brothers and Sisters, good morning!

Today's Gospel invites us to reflect on the theme of salvation. Jesus was journeying from Galilee toward Jerusalem—the Evangelist Luke recounts—when some-one asked him: "Lord, will those who are saved be few?" (13:23). Jesus does not answer the question directly: there is no need to know how many are saved; rather it is important to know which path leads to salvation. And so it was that Jesus replied saying: "Strive to enter by the narrow door; for many, I tell you, will seek to enter and will not be able" (v. 24). What does Jesus mean? Through which door should we enter? And why does Jesus speak of a narrow door?

17

The image of the door recurs in the Gospel on various occasions and calls to mind the door of the house, of the home, where we find safety, love and warmth. Jesus tell us that there is a door which gives us access to God's family, to the warmth of God's house, of communion with him. This door is Jesus himself (cf. Jn 10:9). He is the door. He is the entrance to salvation. He leads us to the Father and the door that is Jesus is never closed. This door is never closed it is always open and to all, without distinction, without exclusion, without privileges. Because, you know, Jesus does not exclude anyone. Some of you, perhaps, might say to me: "But, Father, I am certainly excluded because I am a great sinner: I have done terrible things, I have done lots of them in my life." No, you are not excluded! Precisely for this reason you are the favorite, because Jesus prefers sinners, always, in order to forgive them, to love them. Jesus is waiting for you to embrace you, to pardon you. Do not be afraid: he is waiting for you. Take heart, have the courage to enter through his door. Everyone is invited to cross the threshold of this door, to cross the threshold of faith, to enter into his life and to make him enter our life, so that he may transform it, renew it and give it full and enduring joy.

In our day we pass in front of so many doors that invite us to come in, promising a happiness which later we realize lasts only an instant, exhausts itself with no future. But I ask you: by which door do we want to enter? And who do we want to let in through the door of our life? I would like to say forcefully: let's not be afraid to cross the threshold of faith in Jesus, to let him enter our life more and more, to step out of our selfishness, our closure, our indifference to others so that Jesus may illuminate our life with a light that never goes out. It is not a firework, not a flash of light! No, it is a peaceful light that lasts for ever and gives us peace. Consequently it is the light we encounter if we enter through Jesus' door.

Do not be afraid: he is waiting for you. Take heart, have the courage to enter through his door.

Of course Jesus' door is a narrow one but not because it is a torture chamber. No, not for that reason! Rather, because he asks us to open our hearts to him, to recognize that we are sinners in need of his salvation, his forgiveness and his love in order to have the humility to accept his mercy and to let ourselves be renewed by him. Jesus tells us in the Gospel that being Christians does not mean having a "label"! I ask you: are you Christians by label or by the truth? And let each one answer within him- or herself! Not Christians, never Christians by label! Christians in truth, Christians in the heart. Being Christian is living and witnessing to faith in prayer, in works of charity, in promoting justice, in doing good. The whole of our life must pass through the narrow door which is Christ.

Let us ask the Virgin Mary, *Door of Heaven*, to help us cross the threshold of faith and to let her Son transform our life, as he transformed hers to bring everyone the joy of the Gospel.

With great distress and anxiety I continue to follow the situation in Syria. The increasing violence in a war between brothers and sisters with the escalation of massacres and acts of atrocity that we have all been able to see in the appalling images of the past few days impels me once again to raise my voice so that the clash of weapons may be silenced. It is not conflict that offers prospects of hope for solving problems, but rather the capacity for encounter and dialogue.

From the depths of my heart I would like to express my closeness with prayers and solidarity to all the victims of this conflict, to all who are suffering, especially the children, and ask them to keep the hope of peace ever alive. I appeal to the international community to show itself increasingly sensitive to this tragic situation and to muster all its strength to help the beloved Syrian nation find a solution to this war that is sowing destruction and death. All together, let us pray, all together let us pray to our Lady, Queen of Peace: Mary, Queen of Peace, pray for us. Everyone: Mary Queen of Peace, pray for us.

I greet with affection all the pilgrims present . . . For many people these days mark the end of the summer holiday period. I wish everyone a calm and committed return to normal daily life, looking to the future with hope.

I wish everyone a good Sunday and a good week! Have a good lunch and goodbye!

THE CRY FOR PEACE
RISES UP

Dear Brothers and Sisters, Hello!

Today, dear brothers and sisters, I wish to add my voice to the cry which rises up with increasing anguish from every part of the world, from every people, from the heart of each person, from the one great family which is humanity: it is the cry for peace! It is a cry which declares with force: we want a peaceful world, we want to be men and women of peace, and we want in our society, torn apart by divisions and conflict, that peace break out! War never again! Never again war! Peace is a precious gift, which must be promoted and protected.

There are so many conflicts in this world which cause me great suffering and worry, but in these days my heart is deeply wounded in particular by what is happening in Syria and anguished by the dramatic developments which are looming.

I appeal strongly for peace, an appeal which arises from the deep within me. How much suffering, how much devastation, how much pain has the use of arms carried in its wake in that martyred country, especially among civilians and the unarmed! I think of many children who will not see the light of the future! With utmost firmness I condemn the use of chemical weapons: I tell you that those terrible images from recent days are burned into my mind and heart. There is a judgment of God and of history upon our actions which are inescapable! Never has the use of violence brought peace in its wake. War begets war, violence begets violence.

Never has the use of violence brought peace in its wake. War begets war, violence begets violence.

With all my strength, I ask each party in this conflict to listen to the voice of their own conscience, not to close themselves in solely on their own interests, but rather to look at each other as brothers and decisively and courageously to follow the path of encounter and negotiation, and so overcome blind conflict. With similar vigor I exhort the international community to make every effort to promote clear proposals for peace in that country without further delay, a peace based on dialogue and negotiation, for the good of the entire Syrian people.

May no effort be spared in guaranteeing humanitarian assistance to those wounded by this terrible conflict, in particular those forced to flee and the many refugees in nearby countries. May humanitarian workers, charged with the task of alleviating the sufferings of these people, be granted access so as to provide the necessary aid.

What can we do to make peace in the world? As Pope John said, it pertains to each individual to establish new relationships in human society under the mastery and guidance of justice and love (cf. John XXIII, *Pacem in Terris*, [11 April 1963]: AAS 55, [1963], 301-302).

All men and women of good will are bound by the task of pursuing peace. I make a forceful and urgent call to the entire Catholic Church, and also to every Christian of other confessions, as well as to followers of every religion and to those brothers and sisters who do not believe: peace is a good which overcomes every barrier, because it belongs to all of humanity!

I repeat forcefully: it is neither a culture of confrontation nor a culture of conflict which builds harmony within and between peoples, but rather a culture of encounter and a culture of dialogue; this is the only way to peace.

May the plea for peace rise up and touch the heart of everyone so that they may lay down their weapons and let themselves be led by the desire for peace.

To this end, brothers and sisters, I have decided to proclaim for the whole Church on September 7 next, the vigil of the birth of Mary, Queen of Peace, a day of fasting and prayer for peace in Syria, the Middle East, and throughout the world, and I also invite each person, including our fellow Christians,

> **All men and women of good will are bound by the task of pursuing peace.**

followers of other religions and all men of good will, to participate, in whatever way they can, in this initiative.

On September 7, in Saint Peter's Square, here, from 7 p.m. until 12 a.m., we will gather in prayer and in a spirit of penance, invoking God's great gift of peace upon the beloved nation of Syria and upon each situation of conflict and violence around the world. Humanity needs to see these gestures of peace and to hear words of hope and peace! I ask all the local churches, in addition to fasting, that they gather to pray for this intention.

Let us ask Mary to help us to respond to violence, to conflict and to war, with the power of dialogue, reconciliation and love. She is our mother: may she help us to find peace; all of us are her children! Help us, Mary, to overcome this most difficult moment and to dedicate ourselves each day to building in every situation an authentic culture of encounter and peace. Mary, Queen of Peace, pray for us!

Mary Queen of Peace, pray for us! Mary, Queen of Peace, pray for us!

Dear brothers and sisters, Vladimir Ghika, a diocesan priest, was beatified yesterday in Bucharest. He was born in Istanbul and died a martyr in Bucharest in 1954. In Messina instead the beatification of Antonio Franco will take place tomorrow. This Prelate Ordinary of Santa Lucia del Mela lived between the sixteenth and seventeenth centuries. Let us give thanks to God for these exemplary Gospel witnesses! . . .

The Lord makes us feel his tenderness through Mary! Today, on the sixtieth anniversary of the tears shed by Our Lady, let us be united with all the faithful of Syracuse.

I greet with affection all the Romans and pilgrims present, and in particular the young people from so many of the world's countries: work hard, work hard to get to know each other, to face each other, to put projects into practice together! This will build a future of peace!

And today let us go home with this desire to pray for peace. I expect you next Saturday at seven o'clock in the evening!

I wish you all a good Sunday and a good lunch. Goodbye!

ACCEPTANCE, CELEBRATION, AND MISSION

Dear Brothers and Sisters, good morning!

We are resuming the series of our catecheses after the August holidays, but today I would like to talk to you about my journey to Brazil for the World Youth Day. More than a month has passed but I think it important to go back to this event, and the distance in time enables us to get a better grasp of its meaning.

First of all I want to thank the Lord because it is he who directed everything with his Providence. Since I come from the Americas it was a beautiful gift! And for this I also thank Our Lady of Aparecida, who accompanied

27

this whole journey. I made the pilgrimage to Brazil's important national shrine and its venerable image was ever present on the dais of WYD. I was very glad about this because Our Lady of Aparecida is not only extremely important to the history of the Church in Brazil but also to the whole of Latin America. In Aparecida we Bishops of Latin America and of the Caribbean had celebrated a General Assembly with Pope Benedict: it was a highly significant step on the pastoral journey in this part of the world, where most of the Catholic Church's faithful live.

Although I have already done so, I wish to renew my thanks to all the civil and ecclesiastical authorities, to the volunteers, to the security forces. to the parish communities of Rio de Janeiro and of the other cities of Brazil where the pilgrims were welcomed with magnanimous brotherhood. In fact the hospitality of the Brazilian families and parishes was one of the most beautiful features of this WYD. Good people these Brazilians! Good people! They truly have a great heart. Going on pilgrimage always entails hardships but being welcomed helps one to get the better of them and indeed turns them into opportunities for acquaintance and friendship. Bonds are forged that subsequently endure, especially in prayer. In this way too the Church develops throughout the world as a network of true friendships in Jesus Christ, a net which as it catches you sets you free. Hence, *hospitality*: and this is the first word that results from the experience of the visit to Brazil. Hospitality!

Another word that sums it up can be *celebration*. The WYD is always a festive celebration because a real celebration is when a city is filled with young people who walk through the streets holding the flags of the whole world greeting each other, embracing each other. It is a sign for all, not only for believers. However, then there is the greater celebration which is the feast of faith, when together we praise the Lord, sing, listen to the word of God, remain in the silence of worship: all this is the culmination of the WYD, it is the true purpose of this important pilgrimage and is lived in a special way in the great Prayer Vigil on the Saturday evening and in the closing Mass. So: this is the great celebration, the celebration of faith and of brotherhood which begins in this world and will never come to an end. However it is only possible with the Lord! Without God's love there is no true celebration for man!

Hospitality, celebration—but a third element cannot be omitted: *mission*. This WYD was marked by a missionary theme: "Go . . . and make disciples of all nations." We heard Jesus' words: it is the mission that he gives to everyone! This is the mandate the Risen Christ gave to his disciples: "Go," go out of yourselves, go out of every form of closure to bring the light and love of the Gospel

Without God's love there is no true celebration for man!

to everyone, to the very ends of existence! And it was precisely this mandate of Jesus that I entrusted to the young people who filled the beach of Copacabana as far as the eye could see. A symbolic place, the shore of the ocean, reminiscent of the shore of the Sea of Galilee. Yes, for today too the Lord repeats: "Go . . . ," and he adds: "I am with you, always." This is fundamental! Only *with Christ* can we bear the Gospel. Without him we can do nothing—he himself said so (cf. Jn 15:5). Whereas with him, united with him we can do so much. And a boy, a girl who in the eyes of the world counts for little or nothing, in God's eyes is an apostle of the Kingdom, is a hope for

....

Only *with Christ* can we bear the Gospel. Without him we can do nothing— he himself said so.

God! I would like to ask all young people forcefully, but I don't know if there are any young people in the Square today. Are there any young people in the Square? There are a few! I would like to ask all of you forcefully: do you want to be a hope for God? Do you yourselves want to be a hope? [*youth: "yes!"*]. Do you want to be a hope for the Church? [*youth: "yes!"*]. A young heart that welcomes Christ's love becomes hope for others, it is an immense force! But you, boys and girls, all young people, you must transform us and yourselves into hope!

Open the doors to a new world of hope. This is your task. Do you want to be hope for us all? [*youth: "yes!"*]. Let us think of the meaning of that multitude of young people who encountered the Risen Christ in Rio de Janeiro and who bring his love to everyday life, who live it and communicate it. They are not going to end up in the newspapers because they don't perpetrate acts of violence, they don't give rise to scandal and so they don't make news. Yet if they stay united to Jesus they build his Kingdom, they build brotherhood, sharing, works of mercy, they are a powerful force to make the world more just and more beautiful, to transform it! I would now like to ask the young men and women who are here in the Square: do you have the courage to take up this challenge? [*youth: "yes!"*]. Do you have the courage or not? I did not hear very well ... [*youth: "yes!"*]. Are you ready to be this force of love and mercy that is brave enough to want to transform the world? [*youth: "yes!"*].

Dear friends, the experience of WYD reminds us of history's truly great piece of news: the Good News. Even if it is not splashed across the newspapers and does not appear on television we are loved by God who is our Father and who sent his Son Jesus to make himself close to each one of us and to save us. He sent Jesus to save us, to forgive all of us, for he always forgives: he always pardons because he is good and merciful. Remember: hospitality, celebration and mission. Three words: hospitality, celebration and mission. May these words not only be a memory of what happened in Rio but may they also be the soul of our life and of the life of our communities.

I offer an affectionate greeting to all the English-speaking pilgrims and visitors present at today's Audience . . . May your stay in the Eternal City confirm you in love for our Lord and his Church. God bless you all!

I address an affectionate thought to the women religious who are here, and likewise to the *young people*, the *sick* and the *newlyweds*. I urge each one to welcome increasingly God's love, the source and cause of our true joy. We must share this love that changes life, especially with the weakest and neediest people. The love of God changes life! It changes all of us, it makes us good, happier people. Do not forget that in spreading divine charity each one of us contributes to building a more just and solidary world.

Next Saturday we shall be celebrating together a special Day of Fasting and Prayer for Peace in Syria, in the Middle East and throughout the world. It is for peace in our hearts too, because peace begins in the heart! I renew my invitation to the whole Church to live this day intensely and from this moment I express my gratitude to other Christian brothers and sisters, to brothers and sisters of other religions and to the men and women of good will who wish to join us at this event in the places and ways that are proper to them. I urge the faithful of Rome and pilgrims in particular to take part in the Prayer Vigil, here, in St. Peter's Square at 7:00 p.m., to pray the Lord for the great gift of peace. May the earnest cry for peace resound throughout the earth!

SILENCE THE DRUMBEAT OF WAR!

Vigil of Prayer for Peace

September 7, 2013

St. Peter's Square

"And God saw that it was good" (Gn 1:12, 18, 21, 25). The biblical account of the beginning of the history of the world and of humanity speaks to us of a God who looks at creation, in a sense contemplating it, and declares: "It is good." This, dear brothers and sisters, allows us to enter into God's heart and, precisely from within him, to receive his message.

We can ask ourselves: what does this message mean? What does it say to me, to you, to all of us?

1. It says to us simply that this, our world, in the heart and mind of God, is the "house of harmony and peace," and that it is the space in which everyone is able to find

their proper place and feel "at home," because it is "good." All of creation forms a harmonious and good unity, but above all humanity, made in the image and likeness of God, is one family, in which relationships are marked by a true fraternity not only in words: the other person is a brother or sister to love, and our relationship with God, who is love, fidelity and goodness, mirrors every human relationship and brings harmony to the whole of creation. God's world is a world where everyone feels responsible for the other, for the good of the other. This evening, in reflection, fasting and prayer, each of us deep down should ask ourselves: Is this really the world that I desire? Is this really the world that we all carry in our hearts? Is the world that we want really a world of harmony and peace, in ourselves, in our relations with others, in families, in cities, *in* and *between* nations? And does not true freedom mean choosing ways in this world that lead to the good of all and are guided by love?

2. But then we wonder: Is this the world in which we are living? Creation retains its beauty which fills us with awe and it remains a good work. But there is also "violence, division, disagreement, war." This occurs when man, the summit of creation, stops contemplating beauty and goodness, and withdraws into his own selfishness.

When man thinks only of himself, of his own interests and places himself in the center, when he permits himself to be captivated by the idols of dominion and power, when he puts himself in God's place, then all relationships are broken and everything is ruined; then the door opens to violence, indifference, and conflict. This is precisely what the passage in the Book of Genesis seeks to teach us in the story of the Fall: man enters into conflict with himself, he realizes that he is naked and he hides himself because he is afraid (cf. Gn 3: 10), he is afraid of God's glance; he accuses the woman, she who is flesh of his flesh (cf. v. 12); he breaks harmony with creation, he begins to raise his hand against his brother to kill him. Can we say that from harmony he passes to "disharmony"? No, there is no such thing as "disharmony"; there is either harmony or we fall into chaos, where there is violence, argument, conflict, fear . . . .

It is exactly in this chaos that God asks man's conscience: "Where is Abel your brother?" and Cain responds: "I do not know; am I my brother's keeper?" (Gn 4:9). We too are asked this question, it would be good for us to ask ourselves as well: Am I really my brother's keeper? Yes, you are your brother's keeper! To be human means to care for one another! But when harmony is broken, a metamorphosis occurs: the brother who is to be cared for and loved becomes an adversary to fight, to kill. What violence occurs at that moment, how many conflicts, how many wars have marked our history! We need only look at the suffering of so many brothers and sisters. This is not a question of coincidence, but the truth: we bring about the rebirth of Cain in every act of violence and in every war. All of us! And even today we continue this history of conflict between brothers, even today we raise our hands against our brother. Even today, we let ourselves be guided by idols, by selfishness, by our own interests, and this attitude persists. We have perfected our weapons, our conscience has fallen asleep, and we have sharpened our ideas to justify ourselves. As if it were normal, we continue to sow destruction, pain, death! Violence and war lead only to death, they speak of death! Violence and war are the language of death!

After the chaos of the flood, when it stopped raining, a rainbow appeared and the dove returned with an olive branch. Today, I think also of that olive tree which representatives of various religions planted in the Plaza de Mayo in Buenos Aires in 2000, asking that there be no more chaos, asking that there be no more war, asking for peace.

Am I really my brother's keeper? Yes, you are your brother's keeper! To be human means to care for one another!

3. And at this point I ask myself: Is it possible to walk the path of peace? Can we get out of this spiral of sorrow and death? Can we learn once again to walk and live in the ways of peace? Invoking the help of God, under the maternal gaze of the *Salus Populi Romani*, Queen of Peace, I say: Yes, it is possible for everyone! From every corner of

the world tonight, I would like to hear us cry out: Yes, it is possible for everyone! Or even better, I would like for each one of us, from the least to the greatest, including those called to govern nations, to respond: Yes, we want it! My Christian faith urges me to look to the Cross. How I wish that all men and women of good will would look to the Cross if only for a moment! There, we can see God's reply: violence is not answered with violence, death is not answered with the language of death. In the silence of the Cross, the uproar of weapons ceases and the language of reconciliation, forgiveness, dialogue, and peace is spoken. This evening, I ask the Lord that we Christians, and our brothers and sisters of other religions, and every man and woman of good will, cry out forcefully: violence and war are never the way to peace! Let everyone be moved to look into the depths of his or her conscience and listen to that word which says: Leave behind the self-interest that hardens your heart, overcome the indifference that makes your heart insensitive toward others, conquer your deadly reasoning, and open yourself to dialogue and reconciliation. Look upon your brother's sorrow—I think of the children: look upon these . . . look at the sorrow of your brother, stay your hand and do not add to it, rebuild the harmony that has been shattered; and all this achieved not by conflict but by encounter! May the noise of weapons cease! War always marks the failure of peace, it is always a defeat for humanity. Let the words of Pope Paul VI resound again: "No more one against the other, no more, never! . . . war never again, never again war!" (*Address to the United Nations*, 1965). "Peace expresses itself only in peace, a peace which is not separate from the demands of justice but which is fostered by personal sacrifice, clemency, mercy and love" (*World Day of Peace Message*, 1975). Brothers and Sisters, forgiveness, dialogue, reconciliation—these are the words of peace, in beloved Syria, in the Middle East, in all the world! Let us pray this evening for reconciliation and peace, let us work for reconciliation and peace, and let us all become, in every place, men and women of reconciliation and peace! So may it be.

QUEEN OF PEACE, PRAY FOR US

SEPTEMBER 8, 2013

ST. PETER'S SQUARE

Dear Brothers and Sisters,

Good morning! In today's Gospel Jesus insists on the conditions for being his disciples: preferring nothing to the love of Christ, carrying one's cross and following him. Many people in fact drew near to Jesus, they wanted to be included among his followers; and this would happen especially after some miraculous sign which accredited him as the Messiah, the King of Israel. However Jesus did not want to disappoint anyone. He knew well what awaited him in Jerusalem and which path the Father was asking him to take: it was the Way of the Cross, the way of sacrificing himself for the forgiveness of our sins. Following Jesus does not mean taking part in a triumphal procession! It means sharing his merciful love, entering his great work of mercy for each and every man and for all men. The work of Jesus is, precisely, a work of mercy, a work of forgiveness and of love! Jesus is so full of mercy! And this universal pardon, this mercy, passes through the Cross. Jesus, however, does not want to do this work alone: he wants to involve us too in the mission that the Father entrusted to him. After the Resurrection he was to say to his disciples: "As the Father has sent me, even so I send you" . . . if you forgive the sins of any, they are forgiven" (Jn 20:21-22). Jesus' disciple renounces all his possessions because in Jesus he has found the greatest Good in which every other good receives its full value and meaning: family ties, other relationships, work, cultural and economic goods and so forth. . . . The Christian detaches him or herself from all things and rediscovers all things in the logic of the Gospel, the logic of love and of service.

The work of Jesus is, precisely, a work of mercy, a work of forgiveness and of love! Jesus is so full of mercy!

To explain this requirement, Jesus uses two parables: that of the tower to be built and that of the king going to war. The latter says: "What king, going to encounter another king in war, will not sit down first and take counsel whether he is able with ten thousand to meet him who comes against him with twenty thousand? And if not, while the other is yet a great way off, he sends an embassy and asks terms of peace" (Lk 14:31-32). Jesus does not wish to address the topic of war here; it is only a parable. Yet at this moment in which we are praying intensely for peace, this word of the Lord touches us to the core, and essentially tells us: there is a more profound war that we must all fight! It is the firm and courageous decision to renounce evil and its enticements and to choose the good, ready to pay in person: this is following Christ, this is what taking up our cross means! This profound war against evil! What is the use of waging war, so many wars, if you aren't capable of waging this profound war against evil? It is pointless! It doesn't work. . . . Among other things this war against evil entails saying "no" to the fratricidal hatred and falsehood that are used; saying "no" to violence in all its forms; saying "no" to the proliferation of weapons and to the illegal arms trade. There is so much of it! So much of it! And the doubt always remains: is this war or that war—because wars are everywhere—really a war to solve problems or is it a commercial war for selling weapons in illegal trade? These are the enemies to fight, united and consistent, following no other interests than those of peace and of the common good.

Dear brothers and sisters, today we are also commemorating the Nativity of the Virgin Mary, a Feast particularly dear to the Eastern Churches. And let all of us now send a beautiful greeting to all the brothers, sisters, bishops, monks and nuns of the Eastern Churches, both Orthodox and Catholic, a beautiful greeting! Jesus is the sun, Mary is the dawn that heralds his rising. Yesterday evening we kept vigil, entrusting to her intercession our prayers for peace in the world, especially in Syria and throughout the Middle East. Let us now invoke her as Queen of Peace. Queen of Peace, pray for us! Queen of Peace, pray for us!

I would like to thank everyone who, in various ways, joined in the Vigil of Prayer and Fasting yesterday evening. I thank the many people who united the offering of their sufferings. I express my gratitude to the civil authorities, as well as to the members of other Christian communities and of other religions, and to men and women of good will who have undertaken, on this occasion, periods of prayer, fasting and reflection.

But the task remains: we move forward with prayer and works of peace. I invite you to continue to pray so that the violence and devastation in Syria may cease immediately and that a renewed effort be undertaken to achieve a just solution to this fratricidal conflict. Let us pray also for other countries in the Middle East, in particular for Lebanon, that it may find its hoped-for stability and continue to be a model of peaceful co-existence; for

Iraq, that sectarian violence may give way to reconciliation; and that the peace process between the Israelis and Palestinians may proceed with determination and courage. Finally, let us pray for Egypt, that all Egyptians, Muslims and Christians, may commit themselves to build up together a society dedicated to the good of the whole population.

The search for peace is long and demands patience and perseverance! Let us keep praying for this!

I joyfully recall that Maria Bolognesi, a faithful lay woman of this region, was beatified yesterday in Rovigo. She was born in 1924 and died in 1980. She devoted her entire life to serving others, especially the poor and the sick, bearing immense suffering in profound union with the Passion of Christ. Let us give thanks to God for this Gospel witness!

I greet with affection all of the pilgrims present, all of them! . . .

I wish you all a good Sunday. Have a good lunch and goodbye!

THE CHURCH, MOTHER OF ALL CHRISTIANS

September 11, 2013

St. Peter's Square

The Church is our mother.

Dear Brothers and Sisters, good morning!

Today we resume our catecheses on the Church in this Year of Faith. Among the images that the Second Vatican Council chose to help us understand the nature of the Church better, there is that of "mother": the Church is our mother in faith, in supernatural life (cf. Dogmatic Constitution *Lumen Gentium*, nos. 6, 14, 15, 41, 42). It is one of the images most used by the Fathers of the Church in the first centuries and I think it could be useful for us too. For me it is one of the most beautiful images of the

45

Church: Mother Church! In what sense and in what way is the Church mother? We start with the human reality of motherhood: what makes a mother?

1. First of all a mother generates life, she carries her child in her womb for nine months and then delivers him to life, giving birth to him. The Church is like this: she bears us in the faith, through the work of the Holy Spirit who makes her fertile, like the Virgin Mary. The Church and the Virgin Mary are mothers, both of them; what is said of the Church can be said also of Our Lady and what is said of Our Lady can also be said of the Church! Certainly faith is a personal act: "I believe," I personally respond to God who makes himself known and wants to enter into friendship with me (cf. *Lumen Fidei*, no. 39). But the faith I receive from others, within a family, within a community that teaches me to say "I believe," "we believe." A Christian is not an island! We do not become Christians in a laboratory, we do not become Christians alone and by our own effort, since the faith is a gift, it is a gift from God given to us in the Church and through the Church. And the Church gives us the life of faith in Baptism: that is the moment in which she gives birth to us as children of God, the moment she gives us the life of God, she engenders us as a mother would. If you go to the Baptistery of St. John Lateran, beside the Pope's Cathedral, inside it there is an inscription in Latin which reads more or less: "Here is born a people of divine lineage, generated by the Holy Spirit who makes these waters life-giving;

46

Mother Church gives birth to her children within these waves." This makes us understand something important: our taking part in the Church is not an exterior or formal fact, it is not filling out a form they give us; it is an interior and vital act; one does not belong to the Church as one belongs to a society, to a party or to any other organization. The bond is vital, like the bond you have with your mother, because, as St. Augustine says, "The Church is truly the mother of Christians" (*De moribus Ecclesiae*, I, 30, 62-63: PL 32, 1336). Let us ask ourselves: how do I see the Church? As I am grateful to my parents for giving me life, am I grateful to the Church for generating me in the faith through Baptism? How many Christians remember the date of their Baptism? I would like to ask you here, but each of you respond in your heart: how many of you remember the date of your Baptism? A few people

I would like to ask you here, but each of you respond in your heart: how many of you remember the date of your Baptism?

raise their hands, but many others do not remember! But the date of your Baptism is the day of our birth in the Church, the date on which our mother Church gave us life! And now I leave you with some homework. When you go home today, go and find out what the date of your

Baptism is, and then celebrate it, thank the Lord for this gift. Are you going to do it? Do we love the Church as we love our mothers, also taking into account her defects? All mothers have defects, we all have defects, but when we speak of our mother's defects we gloss over them, we love her as she is. And the Church also has her defects: but we love her just as a mother. Do we help her to be more beautiful, more authentic, more in harmony with the Lord? I leave you with these questions, but don't forget your homework: go find the date of your Baptism, carry it in your heart and celebrate it.

2. A mother does not stop at just giving life; with great care she helps her children grow, gives them milk, feeds them, teaches them the way of life, accompanies them always with her care, with her affection, with her love, even when they are grown up. And in this she also knows to correct them, to forgive them and understand them. She knows how to be close to them in sickness and in suffering. In a word, a good mother helps her children to come of themselves, and not to remain comfortably under her motherly wings, like a brood of chicks under the wings of the broody hen. The Church like a good mother does the same thing: she accompanies our development by transmitting to us the Word of God, which is a light that directs the path of Christian life; she administers the Sacraments. She nourishes us with the Eucharist, she brings us the forgiveness of God through the Sacrament of Penance, she helps us in moments of

sickness with the Anointing of the sick. The Church accompanies us throughout our entire life of faith, throughout the whole of our Christian life. We can then ask ourselves other questions: what is my relationship with the Church? Do I feel like she is my mother who helps me grow as a Christian? Do I participate in the life of the Church, do I feel part of it? Is my relationship a formal or a vital relationship?

3. A third brief thought. In the first centuries of the Church, one thing was very clear: the Church, while being the mother of Christians, while "making" Christians, is also "made" by them. The Church is not distinct from us, but should be seen as the totality of believers, as the "we" of Christians: I, you, we all are part of the Church. St. Jerome wrote: "The

The Church, while being the mother of Christians, while "making" Christians, is also "made" by them.

Church of Christ is nothing other than the souls of those who believe in Christ" (Tract. Ps 86: PL 26, 1084). Thus the motherhood of the Church is lived by us all, pastors and faithful. At times I feel: "I believe in God but not in the Church . . . I have heard that the Church says . . . priests say . . ." Priests are one thing but the church is not formed solely by priests, the Church is all of us! And

49

if you say that you believe in God and you don't believe in the Church, you are saying that you don't believe in yourself; and this is a contradiction. The Church is all of us: from the baby just baptized to the Bishop, the Pope; we are all the Church and we are all equal in the eyes of God! We are all called to collaborate for the birth of new Christians in the faith, we are all called to be educators in the faith, to proclaim the Gospel. Each of us should ask ourself: what do I do so that others might share in Christian life? Am I generous in my faith or am I closed? When I repeat that I love a Church that is not closed in herself, but capable of coming out, of moving, even with risks, to bring Christ to all people, I am thinking of everyone, of me, of you, of every Christian! We all take part in the motherhood of the church, so that the light of Christ may reach the far confines of the earth. Long live Holy Mother Church!

I offer an affectionate greeting to all the English-speaking pilgrims and visitors present at today's Audience . . . May your stay in the Eternal City increase your love for the Church, his Church, our Mother. May God bless you!

Lastly, an affectionate thought to the young, the sick and the newlyweds. Tomorrow we commemorate the Holy Name of Mary. Call upon her, dear *young people*, to feel the sweetness of the love of the Mother of God; pray to her, dear *sick people*, above all at the moment of the cross and suffering; look to her, dear *newlyweds*, as the star of your marital journey of dedication and fidelity.

GOD REJOICES IN FORGIVENESS

September 15, 2013

St. Peter's Square

Dear Brothers and Sisters, good morning!

In the Liturgy today we read chapter 15 of the Gospel of Luke, which contains three parables of mercy: the lost sheep, the lost coin, and then the longest of them, characteristic of St. Luke, the parable of the father of two sons, the "prodigal" son and the son who believes he is "righteous," who believes he is saintly. All three of these parables speak of the joy of God. God is joyful. This is interesting: God is joyful! And what is the joy of God? The joy of God is forgiving, the joy of God is forgiving! The joy of a shepherd who finds his little lamb; the joy of a woman who finds her coin; it is the joy of a father welcoming home the son who was lost, who was as though dead and has come back to life, who has come home. Here is the entire Gospel! Here! The whole Gospel, all of Christianity, is here! But make sure that it is not sentiment, it is not being a "do-gooder"! On the contrary, mercy is the true force that can save man and the world from the "cancer" that is sin, moral evil, spiritual evil. Only love fills the void, the negative chasms that evil opens in hearts and in history. Only love can do this, and this is God's joy!

Jesus is all mercy, Jesus is all love: he is God made man. Each of us, each one of us, is that little lost lamb, the coin that was mislaid; each one of us is that son who has squandered his freedom on false idols, illusions of happiness, and has lost everything. But God does not forget us, the Father never abandons us. He is a patient father, always waiting for us! He respects our freedom, but he remains faithful forever. And when we come back to him, he welcomes us like children into his house, for he never ceases, not for one instant, to wait for us with love. And his heart rejoices over every child who returns. He is celebrating

Only love fills the void, the negative chasms that evil opens in hearts and in history. Only love can do this, and this is God's joy!

because he is joy. God has this joy, when one of us sinners goes to him and asks his forgiveness.

What is the danger? It is that we presume we are righteous and judge others. We also judge God, because we think that he should punish sinners, condemn them to death, instead of forgiving. So "yes" then we risk staying outside the Father's house! Like the older brother in the parable, who rather than being content that his brother has returned, grows angry with the father who welcomes him and celebrates. If in our heart there is no mercy, no joy of forgiveness, we are not in communion with God, even if we observe all of his precepts, for it is love that saves, not the practice of precepts alone. It is love of God and neighbor that brings fulfilment to all the Commandments. And this is the love of God, his joy: forgiveness. He waits for us always! Maybe someone has some heaviness in his heart: "But, I did this, I did that. . . ." He expects you! He is your father: he waits for you always!

If we live according to the law "an eye for an eye, a tooth for a tooth," we will never escape from the spiral of evil. The evil one is clever, and deludes us into thinking that with our human justice we can save ourselves and save the world! In reality, only the justice of God can save us! And the justice of God is revealed in the Cross: the Cross is the judgment of God on us all and on this world. But how does God judge us? By giving his life for us! Here is the supreme act of justice that defeated the

54

prince of this world once and for all; and this supreme act of justice is the supreme act of mercy. Jesus calls us all to follow this path: "Be merciful, even as your Father is merciful" (Lk 6:36). I now ask of you one thing. In silence, let's all think . . . everyone think of a person with whom we are annoyed, with whom we are angry, someone we do not like. Let us think of that person and in silence, at this moment, let us pray for this person and let us become merciful with this person. [*silent prayer*].

Let us now invoke the intercession of Mary, Mother of Mercy.

Dear brothers and sisters, yesterday in Argentina, Blessed José Gabriel Brochero was proclaimed Blessed, a priest of the Diocese of Córdoba, born in 1840 and died in 1914. Inspired by the love of Christ, he dedicated himself entirely to his flock, to lead everyone to the Kingdom of God, with immense mercy and zeal for souls. He stayed with the people, and sought to lead many to the spiritual exercises. He would travel kilometer after kilometer, crossing mountains on his mule whom he called "Facciabrutta" ("ugly-face"), because it wasn't beautiful. He would even go in the rain, he was brave! But you too, in this rain, are here, you are brave. Well done! In the end, this Blessed was blind and a leper, but full of joy, the joy of the Good Shepherd, the joy of the merciful Shepherd! . . .

I greet with affection all the pilgrims present here today: families, parish groups and young people. . . .

I wish everyone a good Sunday and good lunch. Goodbye, until we see each other again!

THE CHURCH IS MOTHER

September 18, 2013

St. Peter's Square

Dear Brothers and Sisters, good morning!

Today I am returning to the image of the Church as mother. I am extremely fond of this image of the Church as mother. For this reason I wish to return to it, because I feel that this image not only tells us what the Church is like but also what face the Church—this Mother Church of ours—should increasingly have.

Following what I said last Wednesday I would like to stress three things, still looking at our own mothers, at all they do, at all they experience, at all they suffer for their children. I ask myself: what does a mother do?

1. First of all, she teaches how to walk through life, she teaches the right path to take through life, she knows

how to guide her children, she always tries to point out to them the right path in life for growing up and becoming adults. And she does so with tenderness, affection, and love, even when she is trying to straighten out our path because we are going a little astray in life or are taking roads that lead to an abyss. A mother knows what's important for a child to enable him to walk the right way through life. Moreover she did not learn it from books but from her own heart. The university of mothers is their heart! They learn there how to bring up their children.

The Church does the same thing: she gives our life direction, she instructs us so that we can follow the right path. Let us think of the Ten Commandments: they point us to the road to take in order to mature, to anchor our behavior. They result from the tenderness and from the very love of God who has given them to us. You may say to me: but they are orders! They are a series of 'nos'! I would like to ask you to read them—perhaps you have more or less forgotten them—and then think about them in a positive way. You will see that they concern the way we behave to God, to self and to others, exactly what a mother teaches us in order to live correctly. They ask us not to make ourselves material idols that subsequently enslave us. They ask us to remember God, to show our parents respect, to be honest, to respect others. . . . Try to see the commandments in this way and to think of them as though they were the words, the teachings that a mother gives in order to live the best way. A mother never teaches what is evil, she only wants the good of her children and so does the Church.

2. Secondly, I want to tell you: when a child grows up, becomes an adult, he chooses his path, assumes his responsibilities, stands on his own two feet, does what he likes and at times he can also go off course, some accident occurs. A mother has the patience to continue to accompany her children, always and in every situation. It is the force of her love that impels her; a mother can follow her children on their way with discretion and tenderness and, even when they go astray, always finds a way to understand them, to be close, to help. We—in my region—say that a mother knows how to "dar la cara." What does this mean? It means that a mother knows how to "face the facts" regarding her children, in other words she is always motivated to defend them. I am thinking of the mothers who suffer for their children in prison or in difficult situations: they do not question whether or not their children are guilty, they keep on loving them.

> **A mother can follow her children on their way with discretion and tenderness and, even when they go astray, always finds a way to understand them, to be close, to help.**

Mothers often suffer humiliation, but they are not afraid, they never cease to give of themselves.

This is how the Church is. She is a merciful mother who understands, who has always sought to help and encourage even those of her children who have erred or are erring; she never closes the door to home. She does not judge but offers God's forgiveness, she offers his love which invites even those of her children who have fallen into a deep abyss to continue on their way. The Church is not afraid to enter their darkness to give them hope; nor is the Church afraid to enter our darkness when we are in the dark night of our soul and our conscience to give us hope! Because the Church is mother!

3. A last thought: for her children a mother is also able to ask and knock at every door, without calculation; she does so out of love. And I think of how mothers can also and especially knock at the door of God's heart! Mothers say so many prayers for their children, especially for the weaker ones, for those in the greatest need or who have gone down dangerous or erroneous paths in life. A few weeks ago I celebrated Mass in the Church of St. Augustine, here in Rome, where the relics of St. Monica, his mother, are preserved. How many prayers that holy mother raised to God for her son, and how many tears she shed! I am thinking of you, dear mothers: how often you pray for your children, never tiring! Continue to pray and to entrust them to God; he has a great heart! Knock at God's heart with prayers for your children.

The Church does this too: with prayers she puts in the Lord's hands all the situations of her children. Let us trust in the power of the prayer of Mother Church: the Lord is not indifferent. He always knows how to amaze us when we least expect it, as Mother Church knows!

These were the thoughts I wanted to share with you today: let us see the Church as a good mother who points out to us the way through life, who is always patient, merciful, understanding and who knows how to put us in God's hands.

* * *

I offer an affectionate greeting to all the English-speaking pilgrims and visitors present at today's Audience. . . . May Jesus Christ confirm you in faith and make you witnesses of his love and mercy to all people. May God bless you!

I address an affectionate greeting to the men and women religious present here . . . as I urge them to a renewed impulse in their evangelizing work, especially in the outskirts of existence.

Lastly I greet the *young people*, the *sick* and the *newlyweds*: dear friends, may friendship with Jesus be for all of you a source of hope and an inspiring reason for all your decisions.

Every year on September 21 the United Nations celebrates the "International Day of Peace," and the World Council of Churches appeals to its members to pray for peace on that day. I ask Catholics across the world to join the other Christians to continue to implore from God the gift of peace in the most troubled places on our globe. May peace, a gift of Jesus, always dwell in our hearts and inform all the resolutions and actions of the leaders of nations and all people of good will. Let us all commit ourselves to encourage efforts for a diplomatic and political solution to the worrying hotbeds of war. My thoughts go especially to the beloved people of Syria, whose human tragedy can only be resolved through dialogue and negotiation and with respect for justice and for the dignity of every person, particularly the weakest and most vulnerable.

TRUE CHILDREN OF MARY AND OF THE CHURCH

SEPTEMBER 22, 2013

SQUARE IN FRONT OF THE SHRINE OF OUR LADY OF

BONARIA, CAGLIARI

Dear Brothers and Sisters,

Before concluding this celebration, I greet affectionately, in particular, my brother Bishops of Sardinia, whom I thank. Here, at the feet of Our Lady, I would like to thank each one of you, dear faithful, priests, men and women religious, the authorities and in a special way those who collaborated to organize this pastoral visit. Above all, I wish to entrust you to Mary, Our Lady of Bonaria. But in this moment I think of all the Marian Shrines of Sardinia: your land has a strong bond with Mary, a bond that you express in your devotions and your culture. May you ever be children of Mary and of the Church, and may you show it with your life, following the example of the saints!

Along this line, let us remember that yesterday, in Bergamo, Tommaso Acerbis da Olera was beatified; he was a Capuchin Friar who lived between the sixteenth and seventeenth centuries. Let us give thanks for this witness of humility and love for Christ. . . .

I wish you a good Sunday and a good lunch!

I BELIEVE IN ONE CHURCH

SEPTEMBER 25, 2013

ST. PETER'S SQUARE

Dear Brothers and Sisters, good morning,

In the *Creed* we say "I believe in one . . . Church." In other words we profess that the Church is one, and this Church by her nature is one. However if we look at the Catholic Church in the world, we discover that it includes almost 3,000 dioceses scattered over all the continents: so many languages, so many cultures! Present here are many bishops from many diverse cultures, from many countries. There is a bishop of Sri Lanka, a bishop of South Africa, a bishop from India, there are many here . . . bishops from Latin America. The Church is spread throughout the world! And yet the thousands of Catholic communities form a unit. How can this be?

1. We find a concise answer in the *Compendium of the Catechism of the Catholic Church* which says: the Catholic Church in the world "has but one faith, one sacramental life, one apostolic succession, one common hope, and one and the same charity" (no. 161). It is a beautiful definition, clear, it orients us well. Unity in faith, hope and charity, unity in the sacraments, in the ministry: these are like the pillars that hold up and keep together the one great edifice of the Church. Wherever we go, even to the smallest parish in the most remote corner of this earth, there is the one Church. We are at home, we are in the family, we are among brothers and sisters. And this is a great gift of God! The Church is one for us all. There is not one Church for Europeans, one for Africans, one for Americans, one for Asians, one for those who live in Oceania. No, she is one and the same everywhere. It is like being in a family: some of its members may be far away, scattered across the world, but the deep bonds that unite all the members of a family stay solid however great the distance. I am thinking, for example, of my experience of the World Youth Day in Rio de Janeiro: in that endless crowd of young people on the beach at Copacabana we could hear many languages spoken, we could note very different facial features, we came across different cultures and yet there was profound unity, they formed one Church, they were united and one could sense it. Let us all ask ourselves: as a Catholic, do I feel this unity? As a Catholic, do I live this unity of the Church? Or doesn't

it concern me because I am closed within my own small group or within myself? Am I one of those who "privatize" the Church to their own group, their own country or their own friends? It is sad to find a "privatized" Church out of selfishness or a lack of faith. It is sad! When I hear that so many Christians in the world are suffering, am I indifferent or is it as if one of my family were suffering? When I think or hear it said that many Christians are persecuted and give their lives for their faith, does this touch my heart or not? Am I open to a brother or sister of the family who is giving his or her life for Jesus Christ? Do we

....

When I think or hear it said that many Christians are persecuted and give their lives for their faith, does this touch my heart or not?

pray for each other? I have a question for you, but don't answer out loud, only in your heart. How many of you pray for Christians who are being persecuted? How many? Everyone respond in you heart. Do I pray for my brother, for my sister who is in difficulty because they confess and defend their faith? It is important to look beyond our own boundaries, to feel that we are Church, one family in God!

2. Let us go a step further and ask ourselves: are there wounds in this unity? Can we hurt this unity?

Unfortunately, we see that in the process of history, and now too, we do not always live in unity. At times misunderstanding arises, as well as conflict, tension and division which injure her and so the Church does not have the face we should like her to have; she does not express love, the love that God desires. It is we who create wounds! And if we look at the divisions that still exist among Christians, Catholics, Orthodox, Protestants . . . we are aware of the effort required to make this unity fully visible. God gives us unity, but we often have a lot of trouble putting it into practice. It is necessary to seek to build communion, to teach communion, to get the better of misunderstandings and divisions, starting with the family, with ecclesial reality, in ecumenical dialogue too. Our world needs unity, this is an age in which we all need unity, we need reconciliation and communion and the Church is the home of communion. St. Paul told the Christians of Ephesus: "I therefore, a prisoner for the Lord, beg you to lead a life worthy of the calling to which you have been called, with all lowliness and meekness, with patience, forbearing one another in love, eager to maintain the unity of the Spirit in the bond of peace" (Eph 4:1-3). Humility, meekness, magnanimity, love to preserve unity! These, these are the roads, the true roads of the Church. Let us listen to this again. Humility against vanity, against arrogance—humility, meekness, magnanimity, love to preserve unity. Then Paul continued: there is one body, that of Christ that we receive in the Eucharist; and one Spirit, the Holy

Spirit who enlivens and constantly recreates the Church; one hope, eternal life; one single faith, one baptism, one God and Father of us all (cf. vv. 4-6). The wealth of what unites us! This is the true wealth: what unites us, not what divides us. This is the wealth of the Church! Let each one ask him- or herself today "do I increase harmony in my family, in my parish, in my community or am I a gossip. Am I a cause of division or embarrassment? And you know the harm that gossiping does to the Church, to the parishes, the communities. Gossip does harm! Gossip wounds. Before Christians open their mouths to gossip, they should bite their tongue! To bite one's tongue: this does us good because the tongue swells and can no longer speak, cannot gossip. Am I humble enough to patiently stitch up, through sacrifice, the open wounds in communion?"

3. Finally, the last step which takes us to a greater depth. Now, this is a good question: who is the driving force of the Church's

....

Gossip does harm! Gossip wounds. Before Christians open their mouths to gossip, they should bite their tongue!

unity? It is the Holy Spirit, whom we have all received at Baptism and also in the Sacrament of Confirmation. It is the Holy Spirit. Our unity is not primarily a fruit of our own consensus or of the democracy in the Church, or of our effort to get along with each other; rather, it comes from the One who creates unity in diversity, because the Holy Spirit is harmony and always creates harmony in the Church. And harmonious unity in the many different cultures, languages, and ways of thinking. The Holy Spirit is the mover. This is why prayer is important. It is the soul of our commitment as men and women of communion, of unity. Pray to the Holy Spirit that he may come and create unity in the Church.

Let us ask the Lord: Lord, grant that we be more and more united, never to be instruments of division; enable us to commit ourselves, as the beautiful Franciscan prayer says, to sowing love where there is hatred; where there is injury, pardon; and union where there is discord. So be it.

I offer an affectionate greeting to all the English-speaking pilgrims present at today's Audience . . . May your stay in the Eternal City confirm you in love for Christ and his Church. God bless you all!

WE PRAY FOR PEACE

September 29, 2013

St. Peter's Square

Dear Brothers and Sisters,

Before concluding this celebration, I would like to greet you all and thank you for your participation, especially the catechists who have come from so many parts of the world.

I address a special greeting to my Brother, H.B. Youhanna X, Greek Orthodox Patriarch of Antioch and All the East. His presence invites us to pray once again for peace in Syria and in the Middle East. . . .

Let us remember with joy the beatification yesterday in Croatia of Miroslav Bulešić—a diocesan priest who died a martyr in 1947—and praise the Lord who endows people with the power to bear the supreme witness.

Let us now address to Mary . . .

I BELIEVE IN ONE, HOLY CHURCH

OCTOBER 2, 2013

ST. PETER'S SQUARE

Dear Brothers and Sisters, good morning!

In the *Creed*, after professing: "I believe in one Church," we add the adjective "holy"; we affirm the sanctity of the Church, and this is a characteristic that has been present from the beginning in the consciousness of early Christians, who were simply called "the holy people" (cf. Acts 9:13, 32, 41; Rom 8:27; 1 Cor 6:1), because they were certain that it is the action of God, the Holy Spirit that sanctifies the Church.

But in what sense is the Church holy if we see that the historical Church, on her long journey through the centuries, has had so many difficulties, problems, dark moments? How can a Church consisting of human

72

beings, of sinners, be holy? Sinful men, sinful women, sinful priests, sinful sisters, sinful bishops, sinful cardinals, a sinful pope? Everyone. How can such a Church be holy?

1. To respond to this question I would like to be led by a passage from the Letter of St. Paul to the Christians of Ephesus. The Apostle, taking as an example family relationships, states that "Christ loved the Church and gave himself up for her, that he might sanctify her" (Eph 5:25-26). Christ loved the Church, by giving himself on the Cross. And this means that the Church is holy because she comes from God who is holy, he is faithful to her and does not abandon her to the power of death and of evil (cf. Mt 16:18). She is holy because Jesus Christ, the Holy One of God (cf. Mk 1:24), is indissolubly united to her (cf. Mt 28:20); She is holy because she is guided by the Holy Spirit who purifies, transforms, renews. She is not holy by her own merits, but because God makes her holy, it is the fruit of the Holy Spirit and of his gifts. It is not we who make her holy. It is God, the Holy Spirit, who in his love makes the Church holy.

2. You could say to me: but the Church is made up of sinners, we see them everyday. And this is true: we are a Church of sinners; and we sinners are called to let ourselves be transformed, renewed, sanctified by God. There has been in history the temptation for some to say: the Church is only the Church of the pure, the perfectly consistent, and expels all the rest. This is not true! This is heresy! The Church, that is holy, does not reject sinners; she does not

reject us all; she does not reject because she calls everyone, welcomes them, is open even to those furthest from her, she calls everyone to allow themselves to be enfolded by the mercy, the tenderness and the forgiveness of the Father, who offers everyone the possibility of meeting him, of journeying toward sanctity. "Well! Father, I am a sinner, I have tremendous sins, how can I possibly feel part of the Church? Dear brother, dear sister, this is exactly what the Lord wants, that you say to him: "Lord, here I am, with my sins." Is one of you here without sin? Anyone? No one, not one of us. We all carry our sins with us. But the Lord wants to hear us say to him: "Forgive me, help me to walk, change my heart!" And the Lord can change your heart. In the Church, the God we encounter is not a merciless judge, but like the Father in the Gospel parable. You may be like the son who left home, who sank to the depths, farthest from the Gospel. When you have the strength to say: I want to come home, you will find the door open. God will come to meet you because he is always waiting for you, God is always waiting for you, God embraces you, kisses you and celebrates. That is how the Lord is, that is how the tenderness of our Heavenly Father is. The Lord wants us to belong to a Church that knows how to open her arms and

> **When you have the strength to say: I want to come home, you will find the door open.**

welcome everyone, that is not a house for the few, but a house for everyone, where all can be renewed, transformed, sanctified by his love, the strongest and the weakest, sinners, the indifferent, those who feel discouraged or lost. The Church offers all the possibility of following a path of holiness, that is the path of the Christian: she brings us to encounter Jesus Christ in the Sacraments, especially in Confession and in the Eucharist; she communicates the Word of God to us, she lets us live in charity, in the love of God for all. Let us ask ourselves then, will we let

Sanctity does not consist especially in doing extraordinary things, but in allowing God to act.

ourselves be sanctified? Are we a Church that calls and welcomes sinners with open arms, that gives courage and hope, or are we a Church closed in on herself? Are we a Church where the love of God dwells, where one cares for the other, where one prays for the others?

3. A final question: what can I, a weak fragile sinner, do? God says to you: do not be afraid of holiness, do not be afraid to aim high, to let yourself be loved and purified by God, do not be afraid to let yourself be guided by the Holy Spirit. Let us be infected by the holiness of God. Every Christian is called to sanctity (cf. Dogmatic Constitution *Lumen Gentium*, nos. 19-42); and sanctity does not consist especially in doing extraordinary things,

but in allowing God to act. It is the meeting of our weakness with the strength of his grace, it is having faith in his action that allows us to live in charity, to do everything with joy and humility, for the glory of God and as a service to our neighbor. There is a celebrated saying by the French writer Léon Bloy, who in the last moments of his life, said: "The only real sadness in life is not becoming a saint." Let us not lose the hope of holiness, let us follow this path. Do we want to be saints? The Lord awaits us, with open arms; he waits to accompany us on the path to sanctity. Let us live in the joy of our faith, let us allow ourselves to be loved by the Lord . . . let us ask for this gift from God in prayer, for ourselves and for others.

. . . Upon all the English-speaking pilgrims and visitors present at today's Audience, . . . I invoke God's blessings of joy and peace!

Lastly, an affectionate thought goes to *young people*, to the *sick* and to *newlyweds*. Today we commemorate Guardian Angels. May their presence strengthen in each one of you, dear *young people*, the certainty that God is accompanying you on the journey of life; may they sustain you, dear *sick people*, by alleviating your daily struggle; and may they help you, dear *newlyweds*, in building your family upon the love of God.